WHIP-HOT & GRIPPY

HEATHER PHILLIPSON has published four volumes of poetry, including two full-length collections with Bloodaxe: *Instant-flex 718* (2013), which was shortlisted for the 2013 Fenton Aldeburgh First Collection Prize and the Michael Murphy Memorial Prize, and *Whip-hot & Grippy* (2019). She received an Eric Gregory Award in 2008, a Faber New Poets Award in 2009, was named a Next Generation Poet in 2014, and received *Poetry* magazine's Friends of Literature Prize in 2016.

She is also an award-winning artist, working across video, sculpture, environments, drawing, music and web projects. Solo projects include the Fourth Plinth in Trafalgar Square in 2020, recent exhibitions at Whitechapel Gallery London, Schirn Kunsthalle Frankfurt, Frieze Projects New York and BALTIC Centre for Contemporary Art, and major commissions for the Museum of Contemporary Art Chicago and Art on the Underground's flagship site at Gloucester Road station, London. She received the Film London Jarman Award 2016 and the European Short Film Award selection from the International Film Festival Rotterdam in 2018.

HEATHER PHILLIPSON

Whip-hot & Grippy

BLOODAXE BOOKS

ISBN: 978 1 78037 467 3

First published 2019 by
Bloodaxe Books Ltd,
Eastburn,
South Park,
Hexham,
Northumberland NE46 1BS.

www.bloodaxebooks.com
For further information about Bloodaxe titles
please visit our website and join our mailing list
or write to the above address for a catalogue

Supported using public funding by

**ARTS COUNCIL
ENGLAND**

Cover design: Heather Phillipson

Printed in Great Britain by Bell & Bain Limited, Glasgow, Scotland, on
acid-free paper sourced from mills with FSC chain of custody certification

ACKNOWLEDGEMENTS

Thanks to the publications and programmes in which some of these poems first appeared or were broadcast: *14th Istanbul Biennial*, exhibition catalogue (IKSV, 2015), *I Was Raised on the Internet*, exhibition catalogue (Museum of Contemporary Art, Chicago, 2018), *Passage* (The Wapping Project, 2017), *Poetry*, *Poetry London*, *The Poetry Review*, *Poetry Wales*, *Random Acts / Channel 4*, *The Verb* (BBC Radio 3) and *The White Review*.

Earlye in the Morning was originally commissioned and published in Arabic and English in 2019 for Sharjah Biennial 14 catalogue, *LEAVING THE ECHO CHAMBER*. It is reprinted here courtesy of Sharjah Art Foundation.

Personal Statement was first presented in lecture form for *What Makes Us Human: Anxiety* at Tate Britain in 2018. The footnoted quotations are from [1] Jean-Luc Nancy, *Corpus*, and [2] Boris Pasternak, *Doctor Zhivago*.

more flinching first appeared as an exhibition at the Whitechapel Gallery in 2016 and was subsequently published in *The Body that Remains* (Punctum, 2018) and as a self-contained pamphlet (Periplum Press, 2018).

XXL thanks to my blood & other families and my go-to interlocutors Emily, David, Jake and Marj

CONTENTS

latest technology

– it isn't obvious how all this works – life
goes on but does it go on like spreadable
dairy-grease or more easy-fit bedding?
or does it go on like up-next: unspooled intestines,
indulged false-hope, auto-play: a monologist: your lug-hole?
I say, please – go on – and regret it – I say
life's a lubricating substance it made these hot-pants
go on like a dream – I say, life goes on
like the first rough rushes, or does it go on
like boots in synchronous lateral excitation
before the bridge collapses?

once life's gone on far too far
and not wide enough, we're snagging
when death comes to it but does it
come-to like a coma patient or aroused suspicion
or does it come like a fiery orgasm tableau?
who wouldn't want to get their gob around
the rich hors d'oeuvres after the rich hors d'oeuvres
the hot ménage new flavour the palate cleanser?
or does life go on like the undertaker's overcoat
before they lob my bod in a trough of mud (flooded)?

never let it be said we've made progress
when the options remain
being burned to a crisp or getting shovelled

Guess what?

From the get-go, we went along with the whopping scam. The whole planet looked like food, and all its muddy creatures our handy/cosmic pizza. We ate hungrily, because eating resembles hunting and hunting resembles love and we just loved the heat-up-wipe-clean induction hob. We were hell-bent on love. Or our shoddy but realistic guesstimate of it.

Sex, sex, sex was reliable. Walking along corridors, filling holes with plaster, Bankers Automated Clearance Services, this was sex. Restocking our mouths was sex. Stapling documents was sex. Automated weaponry was sex. Locking and unlocking doors was sex. A particularly satisfying variant involved long-distance chat with no physical contact.

Who am I trying to kid? Excuse me while I peel my banana.

But we did have a trick up our sleeves. Putting it all down to remote control, piloted from thousands of miles away, we could shrug off common feelings like the common cold. We could pump iron.

I'll simply die if I don't.

Duct tape, crude oils, minerals + multi-vits! Anxiety came as standard, or was it anticipation or a frisson of isolation? Quite apart from being indoors, mainly, quite apart from checking the forecast, quite apart from managing the mailbox, we had the wave of the future rushing under our weakening thighs. We spent years pressed to the chest of boredom/waiting, then
> kerpoW

! a crematorium.

Motion is exhausting. It's a gutsy thing to keep feeling the world's movements.

And that's not really the problem anyway. There was something in the brushwork of FuckItYesNails! that reminded us of the brutal interfaces. Leopard-print lacquer was revised repeatedly. Women in face-masks attended to our chipped outer-layers. O THANX! we verbalised, because prevention of flaking was tantamount to love-making.

Do you l.o.v.e the sound of trembling in late September?

And then the handle came off my bicycle, right there in my hand, all slithery! Down I went, nosing tarmac, about-to-snuff-it, alone with a road sign. !But what'll happen to the wet kiss never slapped on his hot lips? !I hadn't been meaning to go on about the sliminess of our situation! !How many handbags I loved and lost! !Don't dead bodies belong to others? Slouched like a bleeding ulcer on a thirsty highway, I saw larvae collecting around the pre-rotten innards. I saw my physical make-up, proportions balanced like an aerated chocolate bar with mint polyps. It wasn't easy to breathe, as usual.

Then I survived. But I hate all that bs. Language is like teeth, which, before we let language appear, were for murdering or caressing. They too have celebrations and die.

A dentist weeps for the rubble scratching our molars.

That's why we get so behind, the daily mega clean-up. Water, thank god, screams like brainwaves and, when it can manage it, floods a person's surfaces with no traces.

Then there's the other side of the argument. Our underpants are shrinking, partly because we're in them too deep, like the contracting continents. After the saturation and the clingy fabrics, wow the circulation bubbles like butter! And melts away.

when did you start feeling like this?

why not try on
thoughts like 'black' denim
chafed from overuse especially
around the crotch where the irrational stuff happens
we're at it again going in pulling out – the hole
before the ELECTRIC bus re-starts is plugged
by an ambulance (BLAST!) – when inflamed
let's not beat the bad ideas let's violently
WIPE the good ones –
let's not pretend we don't know
every noise is an attempt
on the senses – all words
and phrases are too tranquil
to describe what we FEEL
when we look at dead bodies we feel
ourselves what's left of US after
deodorisation oh ffs so what
if I said you were BEAUTIFUL
and nearly meant it I don't mean that
beautifulness is accessible like
a takeaway delivery and how is that NOT
an oxymoron it's the opposite
of POLITICS which appears concerned
only with things that can be talked about and
we're not BORN talkers
it took at least 2 years to talk
about the curiosities we got handed
none of which we asked for or last
except a CERTAIN QUANTITY of guilt – btw
– TROPICAL WINTER IS COMING IN –
where are you FROM? I'm from

my mother via several buildings and
occasions wondering if I've really
considered EVERYone else's feelings

it's not just a conditioning shampoo it's

an experience is not a claim
we're not going to resolve easily but
that doesn't mean all experiences
aren't possible though any experience might be
a significant blow, a French man painter
wanted to bust the system he said the day
is coming when a single carrot
freshly observed will set off
a revolution – an extended metaphor? no –
one of my hairs it's here to stiffen
support for the smell of pigment the noise
of exhaustion the way of falling
that's brought it to the table now it's on the table
I declare my independence from it often
I have no idea how I've come to be where
I am or how days have passed – at a distance
I look at it as if it were (either the
cause or the symptom) me – broken

CHEERS!

it tastes
like going on holiday
in a boat pushed HARD
through a wall into a jungle
where refreshments are an orb
plucked from a sky that ejaculates
salad when you squeeze it

bottoms UP!

it knocks off
my anxious bundles
to let you peek
at my secrets
and I trust a drink better
than my feelings
in rooms that feel hotter
when my feelings are in them

to paraphrase the optimists

I'm inside and outside
it's raining
chilly chamois ridges
on faces faeces heads and headstones
it reigns democratically
with no hoo-ha or overheads
unlike the monarchy
what an embarrassment
to have a monarchy when

CHEERS!

the atmosphere is literally a chaotic system
as intense as downing a glass of hot ceviche tears
it tastes
of all the time-honoured indecent bits of life
very HOT
and unexpected which is the hottest thing
and these are the days
when you can even steam-clean

                              !

EVENINGS

of general can't-be-arsed-ness
when the word 'no' sheds most of its meaning
no words don't mean
NOTHING

after a skinful
it's too HOT even to refuse long eye contact
like being pushed HARD
into a raw sweat
in a sauna but

GOOD NEWS!

if your problem with compact umbrellas
is that they are too feminine
your problem is not compact
umbrellas umbrellas
don't open and close in isolation
they're always close to us
in the drizzle on an exposed lightly stained hardwood picnic bench
plonked for years beside a busy road getting eroded

ENJOY!

the thunderous throat-sting
often gobsmacking
dehydrated membranes
thoracic breathing
floating over the decking
like a toxic balloon
luckily
I'm up for body odours
when other forms of empathy are thinning

or nothing

makes it easier
to be your own person
made of collated emotion
emotion is not a side dish
even if you try to hide the sentiment
by texting between your legs

don't bother

with the plot
by the time 'later' rolls around
the novelty of getting home safely
will have been whisked into airspace

CHEERS!

to the future when
someone else
will have their bum where mine is
listening to
someone else
tell them they miss their ex
repeatedly
like the far-off moaning of a goat

being slaughtered on an overstretched farm
in the middle of apple trees in bloom
in spitting distance
of a late-summer motorway
the infinitely patient and sweet velvet of my donkey eyes

watching cat hair blown into the street
skin flakes too
a blizzard of multi-species dandruff
are you sure

this didn't happen?

maybe
ONE MORE why not
waste a clever idea
one more is when I stop
inhabiting certain parts
of myself when windows start
to get on my last nerve so
strangely impartial
neither tight nor diluted
like ice-cubes that hang there
refusing to crack
just a drip-drip
of revelation
revving up about to
PLEASE
let the feeling of life
LET GO
of me

Take Spanking White Pants

Millions love and die wearing them. A couple
of blunt pairs twirl on the rotary airer right now.
Streaks in their hollow core. As in, they've seen
better days. But, looking out, it could be
almost warm, breezing uneasily.
It really seems as if all time has passed
relative to our condition, skins on tight.
Forgive me, love me, make me new.

You get what's getting got at.
Far too much is the starting point for not much.
The pants self-sauté or the sky bashes them
with clues. The secret is slow, slow
and prolonged baking. A day off
from disappointments in touch, little accidents,
excitement and fatigue, sore butts and heads.
Ideally, a wall of drought.

Or it's just winter wheezing over the fence.
Trust nippy days, slightly overblown
like the worn and needed cliché, the obvious
where the pants hang out, a routine linking average
but unknowable troubles, laughable in their exposure
in their concealment, to flatter all regions while,
underneath, it happens. World of interiors.

some things

by which I mean everything
is bursting nearly everything's bursting
under the pumping load
of the whopping big-shot circle-jerk
starring hair-dried toupees
faecal supplicants topless jockeys & gropers
    spurting across the clocks across
    our faces screaming across time-zones
    shovelling down sound-bites & sicking them
    over our saddest images
    projecting brute mise-en-scènes
    from their supremo arseholes
    launching everything
        with SUPER
        super super hot super meat super
        scary super hard super wall super
        man super size super dooper super
           moon which is marginally
        more super than a 15″ pizza
      pressing ever closer to your eyeballs
   yet forever out of tonguing distance
like crème brûlée on a stick
   I'm trembly but mobile well
    IT WOULD BE WEIRDER
    NOT TO BE HAVING NIGHTMARES
    RIGHT NOW and imminently
    it'll be too late to even smell
the dead bodies you could be
breezing right through it
and never notice you're in the middle
of a dead-body-shaped hole in
the pounding circle-jerk
you never know if it's a crater you've dropped into

or an outline flanked by groaning meatballs
goading and growing until
they swallow everything   take care!
with your tongue the threat of ice-burn
and lewd gestures is real
                    as a dead body nothing can prepare you
                    for the smell of a dead body
                    except the smell of a dead body
                    or the smell of an unmade baby
                    pushed out on a blaze
                    of blood & other rubble
                    from the uterus at menstruation please
don't confuse the uterus with
the urethra with the vagina with
the vulva with the labia with
period blood outpouring period blood
smells like fortified greens
& a squirt of polyurethane foam
patching up leaks of arousal
                            oh pass me a pantyliner mate & thank u
plus a 3-course protein meal given the nitro treatment/whipped
into clods & nuggets then
liquefied in the dark in the groin-pit
                    in pubic places
                    an egg hurls out monthly-ish with
                    great strength let's regard it
                    EVERY TIME U SEE AN EGG
                    THAT MIGHT HAVE BEEN SOMEONE
                    urging forward with nostrils with intentions with
                    a cracking twist at the end
                    that basically means LOOK
                    at the mess I've made by existing what a lark do you
remember the future
in which you got motion-sickness
just seeing lars von trier films
and world-war history now

take a good look at this seared
orang-utan new police state hardcore digging
animal-fat banknotes or contactless
and pitiless our H2O supply
gacked-up to the eyeballs in place of love
the last frontier of private thought
free suet pellet weekend expansive clouds
of plastic micro-garbage skidding
down a trachea an oesophagus
deep in your lungs   hi kidneys
                rethinking or redesigning the whole bloody thing
                would be a starter (the crowd is ready
                to be infatuated) and/or ending
                all parties except the party
                where you meet your own brain   I thought
                huh me again
        could someone make a primer to pull all this together
then rip it into morsels and rip us out
of this hell-hole as soon as possible
so we can grow goosebumps on any bare skin again
as we diddle around in convincing sexy actions
that take us back to that
bonus time of smoking
extra-legal highs fucking
on the VR hammock paying
to have feelings freely
spending too many years staring
into screens and not enough years
drinking gin & kinky
                sometimes
                I feel optimistic tho
                picturing uteruses shedding iron-rich
                goods every lunar month the world over
                soaking the world over beware
                strong currents bleeding
                is accumulating PLEASE

22

RESPOND DIRECTLY
when the chorus kicks in
WE WILL mount our own bloody hot take-over
WE WILL become bigger and we mean GIANT
WE WILL stain
WE WILL sweat just sleeping on it
    WE WILL get very very naked from within until we risk
        our hearts spurting vulgarly the blood tears multicolour
            polysexual weather systems making whoopee inside us
WE WILL pool our discharge until it shoots from the earth's urethra
WE WILL ride vivid & breakneck into their pricked landscape
WE WILL sustain outrage until we fry off the atmosphere
WE WILL use teeth to crunch bullshit and spew it back in their y-fronts
WE WILL look ahead to eye-splitting correctives
like they're cooking with chilli and rubbing
their bits but a billion times over   anyone
who wants to see a bunch of stuff go BOOM
        and all the jerks getting their comeuppance
        look this way now use your own body to explode & STOP
        their advancing spunking it's not a question
        of if we will all go
      BANG but when and how loudly so
there is every point in the jerks worrying
about us erupting into fireballs
sending the jerks bolting for cover amid
flames and flying chunks though
it isn't just exploding sex organs
massive human-shaped sinkholes
will open up too
        even the sky
        over London here's one I took over London
        is really sinking shrill and
        quick it's probably only moments
        until it becomes a fossilised socket
        mid-self-congratulation pollutants let's
        make the most of the moon the moon

won't be this close again until
it synchronises wombs and hurls directly into us
I know this isn't how the sky works but
there is every point in worrying
about our actual influence
on tides and geomagnetic activity
and our own bodies the only thin
and tenuous exosphere everything spiralling
further out from disorienting to agitated to
full-on hurtling gasp-inducing panic
through all the howls and the grunts
until we're end up
vomming our guts in the ball-pit
dumping boundaries all boundaries
out of orbit weeping relief end up

Earlye in the Morning

From overhead and nowhere, the channel arrived one standard lunch hour, skittering over supermarket tiles and worn carpets and car parks for miles, separating this side from the other side, making both islands, of course. After that regrettable episode, the sun on the other side went out of business and the rain whipped the whole locale until everything in it might sink or be fished out.

But that was over there, where stopping on the road was still stepping on a toad.

Here, you were lucky to avoid a heat-wave pothole in the major tax assessment area. Across the window ledges, rubber doggy balls were left to fade to the same tight grey. It got so parching, dry ripples or were they desert whiskers grew up thickly through split tarmac, a mirage. The air out-stank old milk. People started driving out at night to the channel's rim to fill their boots with as much saltwater as the boots could take while they were waiting a matter of however-many-years for the ground to once more unboil.

The atmosphere was a hard new drama, come to thrash the living daylights out of you.

This enforced separation into two distinct sections, with the sharpened waves in between, fouled with smears of cloud, was like a double dose of a life-threatening situation. In the sky over the channel, blame sat like a heavy smog, which made for poor visibility. Panoptic vigilance was required with any approaching thingy.

All these wonderful, sore reminders implant in your balloon-like mind that's supposedly the here-and-now.

At least the voluminous sea-spray shower feels kissy in a cool spot, like your skin's on a forest floor, soaking up Perrier by the litre.

Continuous bathing risks soft ugly patches forming on your surfaces, sticking around for the future or skin-eating fish to chew them off. But ducks aren't threatened by you in water because you're only a bobbing head. Grab your mother and a towel, some mini meat-free sausages and chilled trunks from the freezer, go to the edge, and get very dripping.

This must be how the toads felt, wet-humping as the earth crumbled.

Once, in the channel, you rooted for sea-grass with a herd of at-the-time delighted, later gutted dugongs. Their nostrils followed you through the panting waters. When they paused to breach water, the dugongs danced as if they'd never seen themselves, or any other marine mammal, dance in their lives. They laid their aching bristles in your lap and asked you to be their girlfriend, though you weren't sure this was accurate or translatable.

Words weigh tonnes with possible meaning.

But there's no use scrutinising memories. At least not with the naked mind. Their make-up is as complex as the beach's lip where painfully unbroken shingled miles and shrieking gullets and the tide pull back on keen seaweed showing off its afternoon light crackling against the ends of the earth so that the warning flags stand flapping and marginal like thoughts you can really trust.

The view to the other side.

Using a phone to photograph your genitalia is the only way to really see into it when the off-gassing ice-cream van touts its easy jingle against the window, causing you to gyrate on the spot, which makes notable no-filter effects which make your genitalia self-conscious.

Whichever way you slice it – the past and present, here and there, us and them – it's always not-quite-right.

"Darling dollies, my breeze, my consolation," you'd said to the dugongs, "even though you'll never feel dryness underfoot, we're already part of one climate we can't know. We thought it was a cautionary tale about our insatiable desire for more and it was. It seems the progress of nature, which is us, is to make things the next generation can break ever more easily, dragging each generation deeper through the shit of its ancestors while doing little to avoid hysterical screaming from any remaining men. Yet the thirst remains identical, for love to continue and be gradually different." You'd finished with several rousing rounds of put-him-in-the-scuppers-with-the-hosepipe-on-him and your voice rang out portentously, in a way that made your skin vibrate, bringing the smaller shoal fish out of storage.

You can never see genitalia as it is because genitalia's quantum.

The new ice-cream is complete-meal-replacement, frozen, with a slightly gritty texture, available in selected waxy maize flavours. When asked if it's delicious but poisonous, the ice-cream lady makes it very very apparent that it is, definitely. Looking at your intimate pix, she adds, "I'd be less offended if you'd served me a turd on a platter" and toots her horn approvingly, hitting her boot to the accelerator.

It isn't the weight of the world pressing in on you, just the shower steam bearing against your buttocks.

After the channel poured in, the sun had barely got up before it began to heat everything to helter swelter, slumped down for the night, then heated it all up again. If only it would stay winter for 365 & ¼ days a year and then, every leap year, gain an extra ¾ of a day of winter. By now, the sky would have stopped melting and a chill would go on forever.

Finger-comb your hair. Smell beneath your fingernails.

No one wants to come back as a cloned dairy cow or a dancing cobra but as a very heavy tuba or as something quieter and blander than your smallest toenail. Licking and sucking at the macronutrients resembles the dog-ends of days, rolled right down to their marrow like loaves of magnolia grease-paint, where this terrible thing thought of as a better life trails the relief that you've never kept track of that racket.

It's not too late for anything to die again, as long as it's kept alive.

Until the day when things go out with a resounding bang and absolve us all of our differences, this side and the other side seem hell-bent on temperature and therefore tolerance imbalances. It isn't a thought you like the feeling of inside your head because it has the texture of IEDs and scratching fingernails.

Crusts of unseen detail whang through right and left hemispheres.

The sun has spread like jam a tough bark across all the brains in the vicinity. Maybe the heat over here and all the people inside it are under a collective hypnosis. The idle mind ought to be a jug for casual vexation and dilly-dallying but the fact that everyone's hair smells of old lanolin and the casein clay walls have released their cheesy odours and stink to high heaven yet no longer attract comment makes it seem that, together, we must be suffering from some kind of eternal inattention for which only a sustained Tai Chi practice might be the saviour.

Particles of macronutrient spatter from your mouth like a layer of edible pargeting.

**it's getting rough for thoughts cut up by conventions
we must thump through though it hurts our muscles**

DON'T START
on romantic love without
taking the gum out
or the gun out – much less words
as bodies that bubble over because
they involve us too much
in too much – not so much
formal construct as urge
to miscommunicate – like
wild dogs we don't want to approach them
we want to feel them – not that
I have a dog – full-stop – a dog
has me who needs a person
when a person is already a gulf
no more full-stops or is that passé
should we at least sometimes stop
to make out

hankering incarnate & the apocryphal sputum bath-craze

Would it be useful to go back to the beginning, rolling in at an antisocial hour by single-carriage bone-rattler to lip-smacking echoes? The quacks here at the clinic, caught gloved and slathered in unctions, emphasise a common cognitive weather pattern, specifically this beige one, saying, "I hope nothing in it causes you to suffer mental anguish or a burning sensation" without prescribing any concrete detail while placing my head in a damp chamois as if this is a patented other-world where the lifelong symptoms waft off like a groovy sedative.

Of course, it doesn't look like much is happening, cross-referencing the stars with their persistent aroma of time grinding down. You don't know the half of it. It's all spangles and punch-holes and your meat&veg and quiet sushi maki could have blown up a nanosecond ago and you wouldn't yet feel it. I'm like, Docs, my #FOMO's gone wild the way it dabbles in outer space. It's hard even to contemplate the heavens without a black-hole robot asteroid apocalypse looming in the background because, apparently, that's key to the whole shebang.

Credit-crunch crime-wave casualties. Magnetic stripes garbled with over-swiping. Walls in whip-hot & grippy. Phones loaded with flashbacks, new characters and detours like a comprehensive record of what goads arteries. The screen has only to sing a timeworn rendition of "Canderel in the morning, Canderel in the evening, Canderel at supper time" to get me ha-ha cry-laughing vom eye-rolling drool OK shooting stars. Ugh, it's caught me hurrying through the smoothy-faux filters like a sicko. Fair enough, some want to lick tonsils competitively and that's their impulse. But why must there always be someone watching? Can you live-feed connect with the idea of God? Don't be shocked at the old beliefs dangling in scraps now toasters are having chips pushed in to set off fire alarms on smoking body-cams in locks that open autonomous tanks with fitness bands via face-recognition that wouldn't dupe a pie-eyed elk.

Wait – you can post pictures of your dinner plate all around the world but not a tender truckload of improved sensations comes sliding in to our beds? says a voice that seems to sashay straight from the sea undaunted by the flexibility of the seahorse mating ritual which is as flexible as any hypermobile meteor, somersaulting under knees, haemorrhoids tip-top. Everything we see and hear is passed but had we not crawled so far up our personalised stalks quivering in our own static orbits we might have spotted that, set to pumping music, we can change the next scene to something very different.

You want my opinion? You'll know love when love's on throb like an embarrassing twinge in a long ligament in a DeepHeat™ marinade. If you mince on into it, compress on tight, it's succulent and nice. Most of what takes place will settle on my thighs as buttery as engine oil or Aeonium Balsamifera as a way of marking time and how deeply I've invested in it. Deeply. I'll be waiting to watch the rain give the windows a good pasting but instead life's dinge pulls away like a scab.

An adjustment will follow like waking from an impressive nap with armpit hairs and domesticated axolotls entangled. Immediately we think of the whole city paved with lettuces, and a bouquet, of how it changes everything on the table, and in the restaurant featherweight cakes so fluffy they're served in helium balloons. When the balloons burst, you can guzzle the innards if they don't woosh-splat on your feet which are arched and carrying you to covet the broken window.

There's the weather, which has, by and large, been successful in its retreat from the norm, skyrocketing as the aeons of accumulated data burst their levees. Bacteria vs electrical pulses. Next up, maybe the semiconscious lakes and undergrowth will get rewired to the motherboard and not just the natural disasters but the whole emphatic onslaught of everything neglected at once will be upended and merry, howling.

People will have to start catching the drift, though its voice is lower than a baritone and the sound is different from what my ears are tuned to and my face like a crushed nose-gay. There's no mention of directions. Diddlysquat is really known about the connections between beetroot juice and dementia and how much life a vegetable can accommodate. Who are you? Nothing is shown except the surface of a woman. Nothing is more exhilarating than encountering it at ear-level. What are 'insides'? Here's how I see it.

I'd forgotten that things can be gorgeous in the middle of tumult and I've never understood the motions of the sun or the tide smashing against your brow but now I suspect both are maniacs. When they get the horn they sure as hell don't hide it. Think of the lifeguards in our big wet greenhouse with squids with 18-foot tentacles where every corner is romantic AF and arouses every inclination to look in directly and deep where the relentless blather of nouns has given way to a concerto of squelching and beseeching the insides of things. Octopuses and walnuts.

Splashy Phasings

Sometimes, at the end of the news, it all comes leaking out
into what's called the living room
as if news has consequences
and it feels wet, wet
that is for a dry day, like drowning in an ice-cream centre
and possibly fruit and a covering of meringue
until I feel responsible
for the outer edges
that seal in the true weather, the true weather
is inside me it has a lid that doesn't close properly
if you could see my weather today
you'll see it's piling up on a sea of hot tears the weather forecaster
said yesterday the sky was squeaky clean turning tomorrow
to generic foam pillows
today here they are, greatly enlarged,
expulsing water violently
how wet the ground gets
when the news veers in from the north
and blows it all down
the towel, get the, get that towel, I'm, oh,
I'm oh, I'm dripping,
I'm partly soaked, as if I'd wet
my pants as if I were a slab of half-eaten pie (baked Alaska) a glass
of icy water in summertime
ice cubes in first they have to be very cold, very hard
leaking out into my ice water the same colour
as my ice water more glossy slightly bigger deeper colour no colour
                                                    the ideal colour
that changes colour in daylight conditions like emotions
or have we been misinformed? The advert said
Hi
this huggy underwater garment comes in a resistant finish
and clings to your body-skin

but tonight I came back to my living room
and found it soaked with news
not nice water-soluble news but the oil-based stuff,
so the place really stank, reeked like wet news
and it had seeped through all the holes
and my eyes, which I had left open, were filled up,
not that there's anything really wrong with news
but it does run into everything if everything is tipped upside down
but at least I didn't pour it all down my chin
like Mum's breastmilk, or did I
my chin is wet my face is all wet I'm wet what wet why not wet
why must everything
go a nice subjective colour
leaking wastefully into these urgent fun-grabbing times
excuse me,
your table is ready,
said the carpenter.
Do you have any water?
I'm sorry, we're out of water.
This is not a joke, unfortunately.
Life is cheap right now
or don't you know there's a war on
you do now I heard it
on the news I listened to the news
I forgot most of it, it came leaking out
like my ruined centre, I wish I could contain it
I wish, I wish its consequences wouldn't just hit &

everything slapped and candied and opening

Many of us are starting to think
with our mouths and what's welling
behind mine is a violent Pink Wafer
riding an ooey-gooey dream-tide
of floating Chipsticks
through an overbite blurting
Iced Gems turbulently somewhere
between bile slipstream and a shriek.
Like an orchestra advancing
is how it tastes, like Travelling
Toe Pivots like at roller-discos
where we crack out stacked boots
& finger snacks for a wild time
on the rink like at violin practice
like my gag reflex is hot to trot
like a roly-poly come-on
when the paunchy teacher pants
into my F Holes, "How's tricks!"

Where's the stopper not stopping
the clichéd bellow at my pegbox
calling on me to recap my existence.
That stuff needs to end and
let's start over with, why not, big talks
of g-force, micro-scanning the cosmos,
outerspatial artefacts, toxic
dart frogs, hacking everything
recent, the ever-inflaming ethics
of promoting DNA mutations,
my plushy solar plexus. The violin
teacher's thumbs are on
my bridge section, the wafer spears
up-surging, a beard at my earhole,

crushed E numbers storming
and screeching, ATTENTION!
(Applaud the Pink Wafer (dairy-free
and definite, even when sopping).)

When I vom
on the fiddler's slip-ons
it looks and smells
a lot like one of us, like deep-fried
child's teeth, like I stuff in
bovine hairballs, cat-gut strings,
rinkydink semiquavers, knickerbocker
glories, kidney stones, the Northern Lights
(but the first rule of painting is forget
what you know, forget the colours).
With his hand on my fingerboard,
with an overweight sound, I'm snagged
on the Milky Way upstairs
and uninstalled in my throat,
astronomic and splurting.
What can you do with a mouth
like mine, if you breathe too near it it
gets self-defensive.

Who made the first vomit
the prototype the paradigm vomit
the dawn of all vomit that splashed us
into the snazzy neon sea
of bad old days recently updated
(hotter&newer in a load of worse ways)
with heroic ice-cream men,
ricocheting pointy death-cylinders
and hydraulic robot vacuum cleaners
like there's nothing between
us&scrappage?

I laugh tenderly,
liquidly, feeling like a bit
of a sicko a very expert sicko
and step back, wearing my face
which is the face of a narrator, saying
this is a horror story. A horror
like gazing into your partner's eyes
over a 2for1 crisp bag at a motorway
service station, knowing his sexts
are crap and all feelings are treated
equally here, that is, bare and fruitless,
and you'll be living through it,
the years of pruning.

Sometimes you don't control
the doors and the fascinating stink
surfs out in mind-boggling mixtures.
Sometimes it's tough to resist
squirting your insides frontwards
because the only way to see them
is as they retch into our massive pickle
of a sticky situation of years' worth
of gurgling like every loud shrub's
been fed to a Nutribullet and out
pumps the gloop again.
(Well, the ecological imperative
is that all junk be recycled else it'll circle
Planet Earth and Planet Earth
is already a lump of cosmic effluent.)

Have you been drinking?
Is something perfect
pulsing back from the dead
in your thoracic slaughterhouse?
Can you pinpoint when
this murder was committed?

Or was it a dollop
of describable sadness
when you returned home
to find your heart
upturned and smelling different
and everything within a sickly taste
and no safety crews on hand
to extricate the driver?

I wonder if the matching bruises
on my inner thighs
from straddling the seesaw
while licking Pink Wafers
and taking big nosedives,
running up chromatics,
and the words I've spent
telling you about puking
are actually time
and how I feel about that is potent
as I seize and twirl my fiddle
and fill it with vomit, an aeroplane
is thrusting and combusting
in my mouth's chemical arsenal,
appearing as a spasming streak
as a result of chafing.

But this won't appear as a horror
simply because hippos
may find it richer than a mud-bath
and I am standing pink-mouthed and opened
and I come from mothers and mothers
and we're fighters all nice fighters
and it's the agony matching us that's wrenching
and look at my face it's emptying
into shoes and briefcases.

TRUE TO SIZE

good news for people who like death

just one blast and seasons are over
      isn't that what the tree means?
            before gifs it was as terminally alive
                  as its leaves dropping and resonating with our spleens

it's still something
      more than music
            how often we think of our mothers, our homes,
                all that's possible with voices

when we think we're in Hawaii we're in our livers
      dying from aftermath, hangover,
            the all-you-can-eat buffet and data

are we still here

making moves on the next world
      while trying to turn the next world into
            a colossal leisure complex
                with slim pickings for birds
                and fewer tear ducts

still here
still an animal
      surrounded by animals
            on a planet part-chessboard
                part-animal gyratory system

where humans bring new kinds
      of death, new uses for cheap carpeting,
            new ways to think
                about death like

a diverting bite of nipple glimpsed
through the artificial hedge
prompting mass shoot-outs
and wanking over wastelands
where men's heads melt like fondue

imagine if your job were to stroll around all day
burdened by rules of masculinity
in poses of strange, sex-fuelled warfare
(all self-respecting norms are a nightmare to look after)

I'm not any kind of religious person
but every time I see this I feel
the fine thread connecting
hot cheese & destruction

TRUE TO SIZE

What if I side-saddled a static motorbike with fewer feelings to confuse the cruising GPS and engine vibrations. I've had sex in a lot of places but not on a volcano until he saw me and burst into magma. My flame-retardant centre was his consolation. At the moment, I told him, we're deep in the mediation of ever more subtly inserted technologies of co-created desire enacting the latest phase of designed living through algorithm. All these high-sugar confectioneries and clone cigarettes haven't done much for my looks or they've done plenty. My face is very me, in use, blood blazing through my everything. My vital life-force! It doesn't have to be lo-cut to be revealing. No this isn't fantasy, this is actual real bloody life, mate, so why get married? We're the only species that wastes time doing it. Marriage – a symbolic and legal portmanteau for maintaining libido and repression particularly in its sagging middle section based on giant wobbling balloons and pet-health-insurance. I can put up with a lot but not blah-blah questions about whether women have got the balls. We're this close to checking out of planet earth and still coming at you with the indestructibly appealing eco-holes we clench in our panties.

TRUE TO SIZE

EXHAUSTED
by my time between the thighs of two dozen lovers
EXHAUSTED

from thinking about thighs
as mountains
hips as ridges
pubes as forests
struck by light and the
sky below bubbling and
everything down there baked
like pastry, sugared over, when the
wind's still searing and the shrieking
sun wrenches bits and makes them see-through
EXHAUSTED

from thinking about
EXHAUSTED

from styrofam popcorn
like this crazy weather we've been having lately
flying forward one minute, crashing back next
it's always the case – tiny scraps of information
blown out of the skies
officials are saying it could be human intervention,
technical failure, time fizzing out –
I don't know where it goes, and I've looked everywhere
EXHAUSTED

from not-seeing the wind
just feeling it finger my
EXHAUSTED

waterproofs
let's blame it on weather, which is suddenly like a magimix
it's hard not to take time personally
      EXHAUSTED

thinking about
dying words:
dying words:
dying words

TRUE TO SIZE

no I don't want softer
skin, I'm more interested
in how to smell good

               dead

my enthusiasm
for going home
to a chemical peel
is degrading, for god's sake
leave me to

               jerk off

my dress
and break down
today's alert

               sweat

with a long anal douche
Mon / Tues
I'm quite fresh
Fri
I'm best before
end of ancient Greece ancient

               GREASE –

how poorly evolved we are
for the odour of butyric acid
emanating
from the sebaceous follicles
of all animals
no self-cleaning

               teeth

the compulsion to

               eat

treat me
like a heart surgery convalescent
be

                    tender
with my technicolour
so what
if my interior is too
intimate to
                    enter
in one piece
or for any crane to hoist
without brushing the roof
let me stand sinking
in my own magic organic syrupy liquid acid rancid butter when
                    bodies
get slippery&amalgamated
can that be
                    ample

TRUE TO SIZE

now the day has begun
in a hard blue way
to get tossed up
on my giant cart of tears

        everything on earth
        is sopping sponge wet
        I can feel it

in my waters the young
spring plants and fish
must suck it up

        along with malignant microbeads
        I have a plant inside me that needs
        feeding all the greens
        and primary colours

I always knew
problems have colours

        like 20,000 tins of chunks
        = 1 6ft-long blue-fin tuna

what does it go with?
the waves, say

        who really wants to live
        in a melted ice-cream revel
        with no polar bears
        reinterpreted into a colour
        just a hair lighter
        than noxious waste
        will we always live

in a time of competition
and allegiances
steaming themselves to
mush

if only
the hot beach lighting were available
for my internal climate
with a dial

that lets you control
the cloud patterns
I'd strip
to the buff and pronounce
my waters
or something
apocalyptically swimmable

TRUE TO SIZE

thank u I'm feeling much fitter now
my inner world has to be hoisted
thru windows like a grand piano
only atonal & heftier

JUNK LOG

how many μg of vitamin B12
until the party's over
THE END
is a tease
dispersed across the globe
              ouch
chickens
today's ubiquitous meat
fossilised in dogs & guts
& in landfill and on concrete
the man climbed on my back
feeling out other deep signals
atoms power stations playing DOG
pollution shooting up off the charts
so hot we make radioactive spikes
plastic sand data junk
whole new geologic modes
while leaning in to stroke each other
              with casually slaughtering hands

I didn't know
his deodorant history
but I told him about the wallpaper
like up-close hazy visions
(FUMES)
the interior the fir trees endless dark skies packet of value bourbons
expanses of rock and sweat your brain a bag of dried squid (I've
smelled it before in knickers at their peak)

              let me keep coming back
to your mouth   I said
tonsils
throbbing dump

low lunging long-tongued
                    DOG
the man slipped in almost easily
furred and spiked with teeth
& I felt like it
a chicken bone
is less a bone than the shape
of a big idea
that floats around inside our heads
playing chicken
staying up all nite in a fridge
saying I'm ALIVE ALIVE
ALIVE or not
& u'll break
many <3s w those hips

                    oh my sisters oh my nieces
the weather will change again
if only for an intimate instant
until it's just a bunch of words
sticking to each other
in a world of connected nouns
& genitals behind doors
off halls off streets
in rooms of concocted beliefs
our bods have ways to show each other we're better
ALIVE
like tossed-off pyrotechnics
dicking about on bouncy castles
bunging ourselves in un-open waters
huddling around the sink in our brains
wanting to go crazy & fight against them
the dreams of glowing pants baby galaxies
why warn you that every move you make
is the other way around
like love also can become a transaction

like swapping one slice
of time for a poky moment
on the rim of a new reality
like a tasty areola greased
with peanut butter the cleaners
keep using hunks of oiled bread
on the doorframes (I've never
believed in doorframes)
erratic pathetic hard and up-close
                    EVERY LIVING THING
DESCENDS
FROM A BACTERIUM
someone says
now u can   STOP
flossing & learning to tell the time
sometimes
looking nice is enough
sometimes
looking is nice enough
until your eyes get lost in belief
(we could be kept refrigerated
that would be a cold relief
                    no more
boning stroking fast-decaying feeling recurring
(recurring (recurring (recurring)) fascinating
how much doesn't last esp when made out of nerves)

more flinching

it came

because I came
through stacks of airport
terminals railway arches security
checkpoints tunnels a revolving door
into the hotel lobby's free wifi HOTSPOT
with Chopin in the backcloth
making everything personal
on tickertape & CNN's mouths
permanently overhead leeching terror
into the common cerebrum where chips
get lodged and served with a side
of forcible emotion because
I already came from interspaced days
and nights of recurring feelings
of my dead dog and grandmother
spreading into all stories in newspapers
of exploding torsos exploding dogs
replacement dogs women griefs
close-up eye-witnesses and already
in my body getting bigger and taking
over until passivity was an absurdity
and wasn't it always and will be

I
came
close to his
WET dog's eye
& a FAT tear shared
animal PAIN sloshed &
seeped in between us –
'darling I'm sorry you
were born a dog &
people notice it

ᔦ

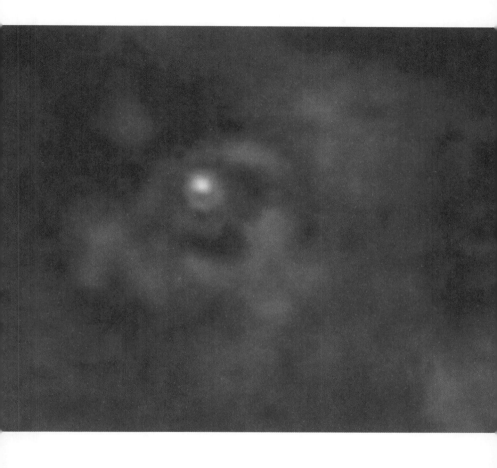

LISTEN

1

oh that
that's just the snivel of an average day
in which every neutron feels charged with significance
awaiting a kind of atomic birthing
like a caesarian watermelon

ready

to begin at the beginning or
for instance
'universal time'
is running
(or I am) already
6 seconds behind schedule

or just

outside Paris
the kilogram is
losing weight
at a rate of multi-nanograms
from the paranoid sweating

or is it

the sky flopping straight down
into our sewer system?

let's   not

worry identity
between the basic elements
we wouldn't want to wear them
out or

for instance

    THE FIRST RUDE BOMBING
    HAS STARTED

with naming
which sets off a disconcertingly translatable
international standard

based on promotional identification
in other words
the selves I inhabit

meaning

(imagine calling the self
for the first time
imagine its first 'bikini wax'
imagine circulating the self's 'clitoris'
(which, the self senses, barely
scratches the self's 'surface')
imagine the self's 'ball-sacks'
having their first self-message
against its first Lycra®
imagine the self's first 'day'
at the disappointing 'multiplex'
its 'aeroplane'/'food' premiere
imagine slamming the self
into the 'Atlantic' from 30,000 'metres'
its 'organs' hacked by 'ice-water'
getting 'carried away'
or just 'drowned' in 'self-pity'
imagine the self shot thru with 'narcotics'
its 'veins' blackening while,
on YouTube, a 'man' is decapitated
while the self imagines itself as another 'self'
or 'thousands' of them
self-sealed in a 'hell' of self-making
why not imagine
the 'day' creeping down
the self's 'complexion'
the 'moon' creeping up on it
      'ho-ho!'
the 'tricks' the self plays on the self
so it doesn't have to imagine
dumping the 'self' on the 'dump'
watching its selves self-seeding
      astride 'rotting haddocks')

erotic haddocks

2 COME ON IN, WE'VE BEEN EXPECTING YOU

like a clue
we found PEOPLE
in the KITCHEN
in the SUICIDE VEST
with the KALASHNIKOV

such beautiful, desperate weapons
their faces

had to be covered
so we didn't fall in love
piteously
with the self-same wretchedness
we see in mirrors

a worryingly familiar scene
we've lived in will live in
the carnage
going on
behind closed doors

being told, regurgitatingly, 'you only get one shot!'

but is it true
you only get one shot
when you get a loaded magazine
& plenty more
where that came from
in the MUNITIONS DEPOT
which I picture in Arizona, right
beside a render farm
and to the left
THE CLOUD
that backs up and up
and up up
to where

are there edges, Bobby?

INTELLIGENCE tells us
to test the power of names
by naming things, for one thing
to name is to guarantee the end
like a starting pistol
BANG

      you name
            it   it's
                     smithereens

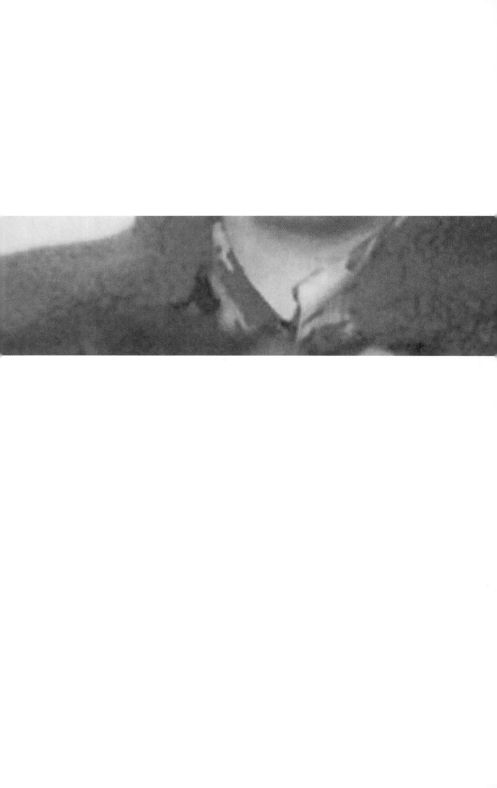

3

do you smell
the hints

1 HEAD
1 SPINAL CORD
1 GUT-FULL

your task is to
sniff them out before
they thrash
the sash window
& ricochet
off our roof rack

I'll make it up to you, darling, in dog biscuits
in the afterlife

in makeshift dark
we can burst apart
any body
& no body
stays intact for long anyway
we reasoned

'shame is inventive'
so said Nietzsche

it's the bomb
that trips
the bloody brain

but maybe not enough
in this corner
of dawn (us)
repetitive and transparent
waiting for a bullet

    .

to full-stop it

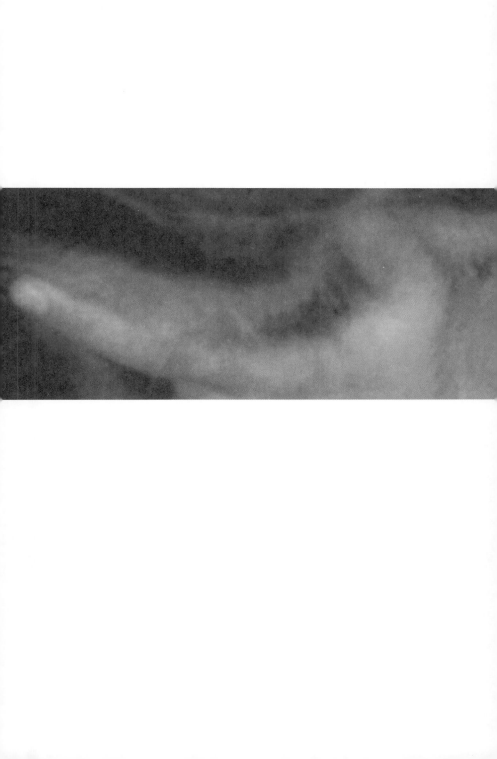

4

I am so indifferent
to the limits
of feelings
I can't tell the difference
every time someone lifts my flap
the unwashed salad
the unheated leftovers
the sanitary products are standard
but bear no relation
to what I expected
to feel overlaid
with various forms of filth
don't you sometimes feel
like getting wrapped in a dog towel
and buried in the hardening ground
under the Canadian maple? Do dogs
need to approach death
and back away from it
like I did when the vet injected
deep pentobarbital & his bowels
ejected across the floor tiles
I was there
to inhale his fur and weep
for my benefit
I am not independent
of my feelings this way
of talking about feelings
has fooled each one of us
                    I'd rather be given CBT
                    by a border collie

when there are fewer words around
my arms around
his only
adored and stinking neck
dead
up my nostrils

throw me in there with him everything is
in the cold
awful and I'm not OK
and without good reason
still here and

feelings

received:

DOG CRATE

thanks to Russia

5

This scene takes place in a moving casket.
Moving scenes take place in locked rooms, in claustrophobic cartons.
They say that when you take a puppy home you should put it in a box
just big enough for it.
Dripping with as much atmosphere as it does frantic panting.
Or maybe I'm reading too much into it.
Until you open the lid, the puppy is also not-dead.
Hear that?
Context is nothing when it comes to breathing.

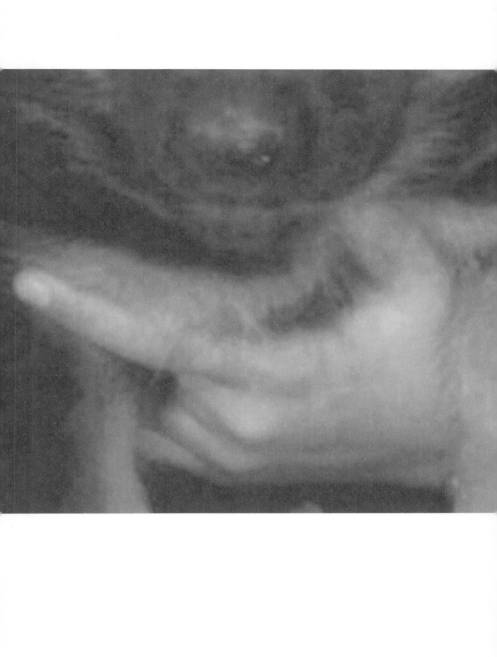

6

JUST A
GENTLE
REMINDER

A LOT OF WORK
goes into making sex alluring sex
is just this and that
but it seemed, for a moment, that a new
climax had been won when
even the sky fingered me
with a slobbery insistence when
we were retching with so much desire
we created a whole new atmosphere
grabbing at sex things /
using the sick bag to be actually sick in
now the shower curtain is transparent
it's a way of saying, "I want you too
to have this experience
so that we are more alike
like a sign that life struck once
in a slippy-bits marathon
that began when our eyes were magnets
yanked to each other's fully charged
crotches at a picnic
when it was essential
to make every enhancement
to our 'connection' by getting seriously indecent
beside the bluetooth wireless speaker system
until even the trees had to dash inside
to pour ice in their underpants"

while I choked up playing the scene, as we lived it,
united by our pursuit of arrhythmia or
satisfying itches to that
catchy bridge section in Chopin
(I couldn't wait to come
with Chopin through his melancholic meadow
(not that I approve of background music
(I prefer to foreground the piano
by massaging it loud and all over
until the top layer comes off in my hand
and the pedal squeaks for humanity
(I like to FEEL a piano as an instrument
of interruption and consciousness
(though I also like to take light swims, to get away
from what I FEEL (today I felt
jellybeans resemble kidneys))))))
which throbs like everyone grieving

7 HERE, HAVE A NEW PUPPY

said the Russians to the French
to soften the dog-loss
but mostly the dog's image the image
is the greater likeness
except we never seem to run out of images
sometimes something in an image
runs through me and that is very common
as is reading about something
that's happening to someone outside of me
until I know someone outside of me
without any knowledge
it is a test for my knowledge
to hang around until morning
practically all mornings are news to me
practically all knowledge is news to me
practically all news is images
going very fast around the world
so we have to them guzzle them
like wrapped food
– hot and on the run –
in one end and squitted out the other
[*pics or it didn't happen*]
until I'm fat with implications
and containing not a sausage

EAT, SHIT, LOVE

EAT SHIT, LOVE

EAT,   SHIT LOVE

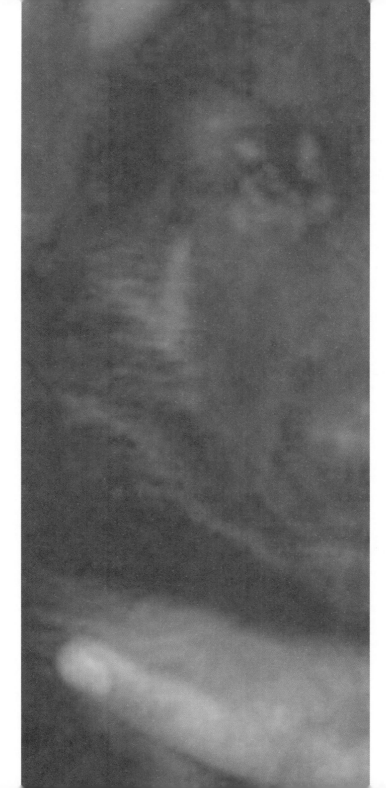

9

I love a good weepie
dog-meme as much as the next crybaby
and nauseate irregularly
when the gifs load automatically
his hairy body
into my hairy body

unfairly the dog
becomes the shape of 2.13pm
in me on a Tuesday

if we accept the world as totally fucked
there's a lot worse coming
than dog hairs in macaroni cheese dog hairs on pillows dog hairs in
rented flats in bathtubs in my hair in my dog's hair in your short &
curlies between my teeth in coagulant soap bars

some people are revolted
by dogs and dogs
are not up for revolting
myself, I am revolted
when dogs are lacking

what if he did lick my cheeks
by which I mean 'buttocks'
which were coated in whipped shea butter
and heavily comestible

it's obvious he's related to a father
he never knew
because we found all his needs
and perverted them
into a kind of inter-species loyalty
or the usual master-slave hierarchy

before laying down the crisp breakfast bowl
of the rest of his days
which gave us carte blanche to rush in anytime
and smother him with kisses
without getting socked in the eye
(unlike when I tried the same on Johnny
(who spat my tongue out (& no one blamed him)))
when maybe all he wants is
just to go on being less
and less subtle and alive
the way life becomes
very well known after its termination

10 [BCU kitchen floor, dog's body (dead), piss]

11

there are things going on
that can't be seen
in the dark
I've been told my skin
looks like an astronomical
surface stretching
from here to eternity
but how
do you see eternity
when our faces
are so close
we can't see
each other's faces
is eternity
in spitting distance
like my lower lip
you're chewing
on a park bench
like a dog grinning
(do dogs grin? what
is there to grin about?)
like my eyes spit

overhearing Chopin's
Fantasie Impromptu Opus 66
the notes appear
as a real thing
outside of me
and inside of me
stopgap
maternal redemption
on that occasion
was I aroused
or sleepy or sad
or too tender
from too much missing
my grandma
in close-up
in the dark
we go too close
to the feeling
parts are
not detachable

12

If rigor mortis sets in
it means there's somebody who needs it.
It means that somebody
is drained and not awake
and deems any speckles of life unusable
and he is dead and dead
all dead in the humus
of trashed bodies shoved down there
dressed in made-up relationships.

What's your favourite part?
Mine's every part
with a maggot in it. Maggots
mean that life's still leaking.

It's like magic
when his dead voice
is nauseating
and I can't see him
so he might as well be invisible.
It's like magic when he isn't
and doesn't have anything to say
and I can't bear to listen anyway
so I just recognise my fingers / all
the injuries they've inflicted while my skin drops off.

What's worse than a maggot
in the EAT ME
GLOVE-BOX DATES?
Does the 5-second rule apply
to something that drops dead?
Is it true he might come back
and crack open a piñata
blue alcopops, bombay mix, karaoke and a pint of nostalgia

which is like thinking in another language,
I mean, how it feels, not what it means.

Half a maggot, the memory of
mange marching across his fur
describes a lot of other feelings
the feeling that someone else is taking up the whole room
the feeling that no one could help me now
or ever whether I was on several edges
my hot core and noggin facing this hammering world
of brainlessness and sweetbreads
was always a favourite word.
I don't know what it tastes like but I know it's terrible.

a:ldskjfa:lkdgjsa
meaning
I'm so overcharged
that all I can do is literally slam
my hands/head/breasts against the keyboard.

Wherever there are
corpses there are maggots.
If we dig him up will he be wearing a jacket?
LOOK OUT
for the milkier, gentler solaces
which for all we know   for all we know
could be the wind
or Chopin's noise (still hammering the background) –
who's seen it? Only its aftermath
is visible what's not visible
is the aftermath of my screaming

13 btw

each second we should shrink
romance by remaking
the thematic connection
between the people we are and
the sucking appetites we become
when we don't stick
with ourselves
we get the drift
we are also dogs
leashed to any body
that fetches & fucks us
with the same quizzical look
verging on so much need
it makes us RESTLESS
to feel better than feeling
LIFELESS

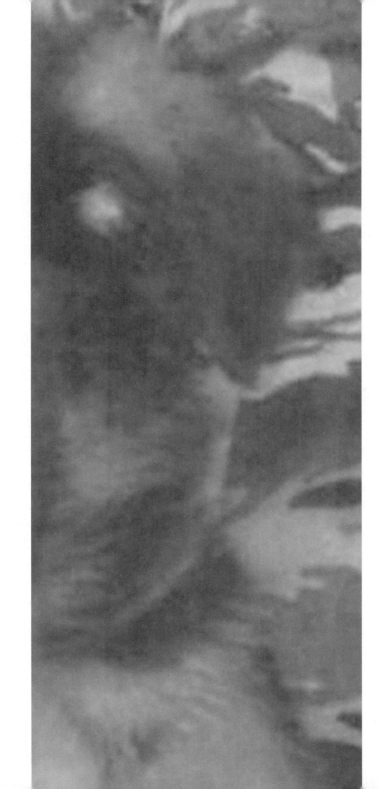

14   HEROISM
          looks acceptable 'on paper'
          but then, so does shit.
          What's turning me on
          suddenly, and simply, is grasses
          picked from the earth's assholes.
          You didn't see that coming
          did you, the assholes
          just come when the worms get digging.
          I'll bet there are some
          nice craters in the field right now.

          As it happened, I had fully intended
          to go shopping for the most
          expensive most wet dog food
          formed of the most tender
          chunks of other species
          in pouches with the same freshness
          and quality you'd expect
          in the field but without
          any shit in the hedges
          and then I got overwhelmed
          by an excessive natural impulse
          in new easy-spray canister, a court heard.

At first, a member of management
gave me the benefit of the doubt
and assumed I was self-adjusting.
He watched the tweaks I made
to the asshole section and was happy
to see the grasses getting attention.
But after a full 112 minutes
it became full HD my spanking
visuals and hand-gestures
were urgently not-easing
until the grasses and assholes tipped
the tone past a point
he and the members
could promote to make-up-caked mortals out for Sunday strolls
in dollops of afternoon wind like an ad for new Hair Hold.
He didn't want people getting whipped up
by the natural elements and then
sexting while other people drowned.
And then I almost drowned! the fucker.
Ironies like this suit the idea that each moment makes its own proportions.

Read more at Scene 10

15 Stubbed toe. Locked door. Walked dog. Poured drink. Locked dog. Walked toe. Pour door. Stubbed dog. Stubbed toe. Locked door. Walked dog. Poured drink. Locked d Walked toe. Poured door. Stubbed dog.Stubbed toe. Locked door. Walked dog. Poured dri Locked dog. Walked toe. Poured door. Stubbed dog. Stubbed toe. Locked door. Walked d Poured drink. Locked dog. Walked toe. Poured door. Stubbed dog. Stubbed toe. Lock door. Walked dog. Poured drink. Locked dog. Walked toe. Poured door. Stubbed d Stubbed toe. Locked door. Walked dog. Poured drink. Locked dog. Walked toe. Poured do Stubbed dog. Stubbed toe. Locked door. Walked dog. Poured drink. Locked dog. Walked t Poured door. Stubbed dog. Stubbed toe. Locked door. Walked dog. Poured drink. Lock dog. Walked toe. Poured door. Stubbed dog. Stubbed toe. Locked door. Walked dog. Pou drink. Locked dog. Walked toe. Poured door. Stubbed dog. Stubbed toe. Locked do Walked dog. Poured drink. Locked dog. Walked toe. Poured door. Stubbed dog. Stubbed t Locked door. Walked dog. Poured drink. Locked dog. Walked toe. Poured door. Stubbed d Stubbed toe. Locked door. Walked dog. Poured drink. Locked dog. Walked toe. Poured do Stubbed dog. Stubbed toe. Locked door. Walked dog. Poured drink. Locked dog. Walked t Poured door. Stubbed dog. Stubbed toe. Locked door. Walked dog. Poured drink. Lock dog. Walked toe. Poured door. Stubbed dog. Stubbed toe. Locked door. Walked dog. Pou drink. Locked dog. Walked toe. Poured door. Stubbed dog. Stubbed toe. Locked do Walked dog. Poured drink. Locked dog. Walked toe. Poured door. Stubbed dog. Stubbed t Locked door. Walked dog. Poured drink. Locked dog. Walked toe. Poured door. Stubbed d Stubbed toe. Locked door. Walked dog. Poured drink. Locked dog. Walked toe. Poured do Stubbed dog. Stubbed toe. Locked door. Walked dog. Poured drink. Locked dog. Walked t Poured door. Stubbed dog. Stubbed toe. Locked door. Walked dog. Poured drink. Lock dog. Walked toe. Poured door. Stubbed dog. Stubbed toe. Locked door. Walked dog. Pou drink. Locked dog. Walked toe. Poured door. Stubbed dog. Stubbed toe. Locked do Walked dog. Poured drink. Locked dog. Walked toe. Poured door. Stubbed dog. Stubbed t Locked door. Walked dog. Poured drink. Locked dog. Walked toe. Poured door. Stubbed d Stubbed toe. Locked door. Walked dog. Poured drink. Locked dog. Walked toe. Poured do Stubbed dog. Stubbed toe. Locked door. Walked dog. Poured drink. Locked dog. Walked t Poured door. Stubbed dog. Stubbed toe. Locked door. Walked dog. Poured drink. Lock dog. Walked toe. Poured door. Stubbed dog. Stubbed toe. Locked door. Walked dog. Pour drink. Locked dog. Walked toe. Poured door. Stubbed dog. Stubbed toe. Locked do Walked dog. Poured drink. Locked dog. Walked toe. Poured door. Stubbed dog. Stubbed t Locked door. Walked dog. Poured drink. Locked dog. Walked toe. Poured door. Stubbed d Stubbed toe. Locked door. Walked dog. Poured drink. Locked dog. Walked toe. Poured do Stubbed dog. Stubbed toe. Locked door. Walked dog. Poured drink. Locked dog. Walked t Poured door. Stubbed dog. Stubbed toe. Locked door. Walked dog. Poured drink. Lock dog. Walked toe. Poured door. Stubbed dog. Stubbed toe. Locked door. Walked dog. Pour drink. Locked dog. Walked toe. Poured door. Stubbed dog. Stubbed toe. Locked do Walked dog. Poured drink. Locked dog. Walked toe. Poured door. Stubbed dog. Stubbed t Locked door. Walked dog. Poured drink. Locked dog. Walked toe. Poured door. Stubbed d Stubbed toe. Locked door. Walked dog. Poured drink. Locked dog. Walked toe. Poured do Stubbed dog. Stubbed toe. Locked door. Walked dog. Poured drink. Locked dog. Walked t

ured door. Stubbed dog. Stubbed toe. Locked door. Walked dog. Poured drink. Locked
g. Walked toe. Poured door. Stubbed dog. Stubbed toe. Locked door. Walked dog. Poured
nk. Locked dog. Walked toe. Poured door. Stubbed dog. Stubbed toe. Locked door.
lked dog. Poured drink. Locked dog. Walked toe. Poured door. Stubbed dog. Stubbed toe.
cked door. Walked dog. Poured drink. Locked dog. Walked toe. Poured door. Stubbed dog.
ıbbed toe. Locked door. Walked dog. Poured drink. Locked dog. Walked toe. Poured door.
ıbbed dog. Stubbed toe. Locked door. Walked dog. Poured drink. Locked dog. Walked toe.
ured door. Stubbed dog. Stubbed toe. Locked door. Walked dog. Poured drink. Locked
g. Walked toe. Poured door. Stubbed dog. Stubbed toe. Locked door. Walked dog. Poured
nk. Locked dog. Walked toe. Poured door. Stubbed dog. Stubbed toe. Locked door.
lked dog. Poured drink. Locked dog. Walked toe. Poured door. Stubbed dog. Stubbed toe.
cked door. Walked dog. Poured drink. Locked dog. Walked toe. Poured door. Stubbed dog.
ıbbed toe. Locked door. Walked dog. Poured drink. Locked dog. Walked toe. Poured door.
ıbbed dog. Stubbed toe. Locked door. Walked dog. Poured drink. Locked dog. Walked toe.
ured door. Stubbed dog. Stubbed toe. Locked door. Walked dog. Poured drink. Locked
g. Walked toe. Poured door. Stubbed dog. Stubbed toe. Locked door. Walked dog. Poured
nk. Locked dog. Walked toe. Poured door. Stubbed dog. Stubbed toe. Locked door.
lked dog. Poured drink. Locked dog. Walked toe. Poured door. Stubbed dog. Stubbed toe.
cked door. Walked dog. Poured drink. Locked dog. Walked toe. Poured door. Stubbed dog.
ıbbed toe. Locked door. Walked dog. Poured drink. Locked dog. Walked toe. Poured door.
ıbbed dog. Stubbed toe. Locked door. Walked dog. Poured drink. Locked dog. Walked toe.
ured door. Stubbed dog. Stubbed toe. Locked door. Walked dog. Poured drink. Locked
g. Walked toe. Poured door. Stubbed dog. Stubbed toe. Locked door. Walked dog. Poured
nk. Locked dog. Walked toe. Poured door. Stubbed dog. Stubbed toe. Locked door.
lked dog. Poured drink. Locked dog. Walked toe. Poured door. Stubbed dog. Stubbed toe.
cked door. Walked dog. Poured drink. Locked dog. Walked toe. Poured door. Stubbed dog.
ıbbed toe. Locked door. Walked dog. Poured drink. Locked dog. Walked toe. Poured door.
ıbbed dog. Stubbed toe. Locked door. Walked dog. Poured drink. Locked dog. Walked toe.
ured door. Stubbed dog. Stubbed toe. Locked door. Walked dog. Poured drink. Locked
g. Walked toe. Poured door. Stubbed dog. Stubbed toe. Locked door. Walked dog. Poured
nk. Locked dog. Walked toe. Poured door. Stubbed dog. Stubbed toe. Locked door.
lked dog. Poured drink. Locked dog. Walked toe. Poured door. Stubbed dog. Stubbed toe.
cked door. Walked dog. Poured drink. Locked dog. Walked toe. Poured door. Stubbed dog.
ıbbed toe. Locked door. Walked dog. Poured drink. Locked dog. Walked toe. Poured door.
ıbbed dog. Stubbed toe. Locked door. Walked dog. Poured drink. Locked dog. Walked toe.
ured door. Stubbed dog. Stubbed toe. Locked door. Walked dog. Poured drink. Locked dog.

16

**HOPE
THIS
FINDS
YOU**

√ just getting to shops
& back
with/out panic attack

17 because

the future
sounds like bionic houseflies
murdering all competitors
in a hands-free / clean-up version
and then reproducing themselves
as world leaders.
Would you rather hose down
yesterday with a stiff chemical
or suck up tomorrow
with your raw eyelashes?
What shall we do
with our ticking stash
of ambition? Blow it up
like the bloated men
who manufactured this whole scenario
in their dreams of being
less boring. Even in their sleep
they are vigorously
scouring our passages. While tomorrow
doesn't amount to much
(until lined up in cross hairs
inside a zoom lens)
our USP is we always clean tomorrow
blindfolded – then, for every hour
after dark, we add another
protective layer – by tomorrow,
we're BIG on cushioning.
OOOOOOOOOOOOOOOOOOO

Sagging energy levels hit early
and later stages since
the PR around *just-getting-by*
is not EXCITING
but the Prime Minister
won't pass away, tragically,
the chance to apply
an exfoliating mitt
to a hi-stakes battleground
here & here
in your living room
where the winner
is the party with the greatest feel
for tragedy which makes everything go
UP
especially numbers
of voters and corpses flying machines blood pressure eyebrows high-pitch
drones high-security fences drug-use incredulity pizza-sales police
presence mistrust top shelf one arm I am reaching for the Dettox

18

what's NEW

is ONE SIZE
FITS ALL dogs'
body-armour with
ballistic-/stab-resistancy
won't suit the dog
but she'll get used
to velcro flaps
feeling instagrammable
like a wrap-around layer
over the layer over
the layers she was born wearing
like a layer of wet lycra
y'know, soiled swimsuits
and then a tougher layer
that leaves her free
to shit and sniff
ammunition
NEVER MIND
a dog's head
should be free
to believe life is all meat & balls & nasal digression
PLEASE
when she bites the big one
from a shot
to the cranium
REMEMBER
you treated her like a cheap safety vest
against survival instincts

19

Me again. Developments.
                              The gin's gone.
                              I know an answer when I see it.
From writing emails.
                              My head hurts.
To the ghosts of dead sniffer dogs.

Have you ever seen a trembler in motion?
A trembler is a piece of jewellery.
                              The teeth ache from grinding.
Stones mounted on wires so fine they quiver.
                              Their firmness was my only consolation.
Once they're gone.
                              There's no getting them back again.

Harsh words are spoken.
                    As if to a dog.
                              The dog's got hold of the wrong end of the stick.
I mention my face because I am made that way.
                              Get out while you can.
This soothing friend will tame it.

Because all people are homesick.
                              This will all end badly.
Contact with actual hot&cold skin.
                              I have the body of a wise person.
A superior achievement.
                              Until my mouth opens.

But what if you just don't have time.

                      For all that lying down that dogs do.

What about the 1.3 million gin and tonics.

                      I'm not drinking to try and forget.

Everything bad that's ever happened.

                      The lack of difference is so powerful.

At first they said.

Then they said.

                      Don't work your glutes.

                      You haven't worked your glutes enough.

Until there was so much beauty comin' out ma ass.

                      I was literally dyyying.

There is still TIME.

                      To come a long way from what we feel.

Start laying the groundwork.

Music is, in fact, the dog's bollocks.

                      Crack open the hobnobs.

                      Turn up Chopin.

          So is the dog.

Get over it.

you can catch me on the

FLOOR / DOG / SYRINGE

periphery of the dying and dead scene

FACE (FEMALE)

maybe my whole life
carting sensations to the centre
mopping shit up with towels

SKULL / COFFIN

(there are feelings for these things)
while public petting

CAR / PLANE / ROCKET

bodies leak it's no surprise
what I give away

ONE DROPLET

you can have
when the vet twirls off
to deal with some bloody business
in a kitchen

KNIFE / GUN

the hug-a-corpse scene
gets deep in the hold
of what I am

PARTY POPPER / WASTEBIN

is what I've not yet been

fyi

21

You can also use your smartphone
to select an element of the universe.
Whichever element shouts
loudest from the shelves
I can't see the ends of. END OF
outer space! has it ever seemed more humdrum?

Yet there is something to be said
    for just getting all your shopping
        inside the supermarket
            when you enter
                the lights thump back causing a chain reaction
                    of never-ending particles I am not in a panic
                        in the supermarket modelled on the
                            glove-box format in which you can
                                manipulate bodies in a separate atmosphere
                                    whacking grim jazzy monotonous and while
                                        scrolling have say not only a micro-nap
                                            but also a micro-wank into this
                                                multi-use j-cloth.
                                                    Huh,

parallel perks in a frigid climate.
Even if you didn't get a good feeling on Skype
there is something to be said for feelings
because there is no escaping
the chinks which keep weeping
and becoming disfigurements, I think.
I have exceeded my allowance
of first and last-minute impressions
all crafted locally and always excusing
themselves under a duvet.

After he died I saw him everywhere
under a soiled towel on the kitchen lino.
And then I saw it was just the trumped-up nub
that lives inside of me
brought for slaughter.
NO to melodrama.
Though I wouldn't like to have people
actually see let alone visit my interior
nothing is isolated in me nothing is isolated in the universe nothing
does not involve me
in many public acts
I don't have time for
pricks in suits pointing fingers at each other.

Everything is getting later.
I could cock up the end
with the beginning
             until I flatline and still in some form
like plastic in the ocean which breaks down into such small segments that pieces of plastic
from a one-litre plastic bottle could end up on every mile of beach across the universe
             be kicking about and linked to everywhere.

22

Actually, we live in heaven.
Eau de toilettes. Nibbles. You manhandling
the dog-food with your firmest hands on.
Aren't eyes are brilliant.
Maybe even better than the dream of grass blowing.
Ha! The sky just opened up, betraying
much more of the mystery of brainstorms.
What a triumph our human state
and by extension the world around us
is getting loved-up on the cardinal aorta.
Touch my pulse to make it official.
Probably just been to the lido, hasn't it, the compulsive splosher.
Remember eye-sex over the microwave.
Remember champagne & valium.
Let's relax a sec and recharge our selfies.
Repeated ideas massage the limbic system.
One non-lithium zeitkeeper, booted to completion.
Until, at some hour, my oomph
becomes sensuous becomes lascivious
accretions exploding the centres over
and over to the extremities.
Then there's manufacturing water from hydrogen,
hyperbole from early autumn,
the retina as a tough/fluffy carpet,
creating an indoor potato farm
fertilised by my own excrement.
Inhale: the high street hums of fried sentiment.
Here we go! – tuning in to the sub-cellular
molecular feedback loop
of our circadian pacemakers
sounding like literally adios.

NO

23

Who concocts the smell
of dogs which smells like
an extreme close-up
of the world oozing
in at the edges.
Full as an ice-cube is full of liquid.
I mistook it for solidity.

The world is too full of smells.
Though it's impossible
to see the top of it
they crawl between my legs
in the shimmering fuzz
on top of the plant
stickers of evenings
tongues held out
pocket-friendly air-fresheners
strikes on our nostrils.
They come at me streaming.

Why the dog? Why not
the dog? Was it only a dream
of soil heating held
and stimulated
for his unique aroma.
It's not a way in
but it places you somewhere
that smells strong
and looks strong leaving
behind us. Hi.

Personal Statement

Like the wolf, I can smell the heebie-jeebies, and reciprocate. Tension invades the scene like a demented baby. And it swells and eats and grows and grows. Survival-mode is a major operation. An adrenalin stab rams into everything along the lines of blackout, amphetamines & hallucinogens, and, in this high, raw state, the vibes get howling.

I went around asking every kind of woman, Do you think mainly of the tempo at which you advance? Is this cable the end of something? Can we form a heap, persistently? Are all your hot drinks tepid & speechless? Are we free to stray throughout & all over? What tone of voice is relevant? Who can tell when what happens happens?

One night I was coming home late with an abusive lover. Isn't life difficult enough? In some ways, love also makes us insensitive. I was young & driving and the sky & roads were popping and the water greased beneath us and we whooshed to the wrong side and I wrenched the steering wheel&us back and into a hedge, upside down, faces whacked in windows in nostrils. Since then, I'm always carrying something. Despite how nice it is to get to somewhere else, I'm a restocked mess. Palpation & sitting meat, gristle. Even the rain has changed into a large feeling. But I heard that terror and excitement are the same thing – y'know, chemically. It's like the feeling itself isn't the problem, only the way we feel about it.

Look. Images get all ant-like up in my brain and colonise & itch it. Whoever's job it is to upkeep the atmosphere has gone away and now the ceiling's crawling with clouds & the damp's made a crack and they're slabbering downwards. Don't tell me there's an explanation and here it is and respiration helps. Here we are and what the hell are we going to do with it.

Mostly, I'm trying to stay with the excremental mood of the world. All the tossed-off elements that furnish my locality, founded in variousness and conflict and things interpreted differently, I could puke. Puke gives a sense of coherence but, at the same time, I think coherence is tyrannical and still struggle to know sometimes what the difference between, say, a mouth and an arsehole even is. Splattering.

It's impossible to know for sure if some wars are up-close or distant or if they're gone or to come or if we're inside them or they're inside us. We've all always been like people on drugs or we are people on drugs. There's still a lot of laughter in the amazingly loud room in which a lot of life gets used in small-talk and what's left out by the data and in by the data. I never could find comfort in the reflection of my own, apparently living, face.

More urgent than the right to be seen should be the right to be hidden. Until you don't have to run because you're steady in the bushes. 'Nothing's more singular than the sensuous, erotic, affective discharge that certain bodies produce in us.'[1] Can we still let the erotic discharge undo us against the plant life? Imagine having a face totally covered in fur. Feel it. Imagine a way of feeling that isn't painful casual or diffuse but tenderised, on the point, while the lateral vision gets richer each morning. Lateral vision is important for recognising surprise, and, as it goes, surprise never comes head on.

Shit the bed, I can almost smell the thoughts breaking down. It's important to put the muck back in the drain and then actually plug it. But sometimes it rides in thick and with such force, it's like a thumping winter surf, sweeping me away from my small selves, and jerking me back again. The endless material gets gouged and funneled and sloshes up & crashes out. It's not that simple, but deep thinking may be better than deep breathing & orgasm & dying moments emulsified.

When can I get down off these tenterhooks? 'Well, what are you? There's the point. Let's try to find out. What is it about you that you have always known as yourself? Your kidneys? Your liver? Your blood vessels? No. However far back you go in your memory, it is always in some external, active manifestation of yourself that you come across your identity – in the work of your hands, in your family, in other people... You have always been in others and you will remain in others.'[2] Everything can't be perfect. Everything's too conspicuous.

Until the absence of an afterlife in nirvana, the years are one way of waiting for the cover to get blown. Until then, here's the strategy. Keep lousing up the requirements because the statute is ancient and it keeps overriding the changes, with barely a titchy wobble. Until we yank it repeatedly until we yank it and it topples.